PEASANTS TO
QUY 1714

by Peggy

CONTENTS

	Introduction	1
1	General Description	2
2	Population and Family Size	6
3	Squire and Vicar	10
4	Landowners	12
5	18th century Parish Officers	14
6	19th Century Parish Officers	17
7	Widows	20
8	Orphans and Fatherless	23
9	Illegitimacy	28
10	Aged and Incapable	31
11	The Sick	35
12	Work for the Able-Bodied Poor	39
13	Social Structure of Quy	42
14	"Progress"	44
	References	46
	Map	3
	Index of Surnames	54

APPENDICES
1 General Economic Trends   47
2 John Arbrow   49
3 Townland or Childe's Charity   51

(i)

Monograph No. 2 produced by the Staine Hundred Local History Society, Bottisham Village College, Cambridge.

First published 1993

© Copyright 1993 Peggy Watts

ISBN 0 9511552 1 0

I thank Jim Watts who has drawn the illustrations, mostly from old photographs.

Peggy Day (formerly Watts)

Cover Picture

The Old Dovehouse in Dovehouse Close not far from the church, which was Glebe Land belonging to the Bishop of Ely until transferred to W.C. Ambrose at the time of the 1839 Enclosure.

(i i)

INTRODUCTION

The Poor Law System set up in Elizabethan times remained largely unchanged until 1834. Rates were collected, from those who had property or a business, by the overseers of the poor and paid out in money or goods to those in need. In the church chest at Quy (now in the Cambridge County Record Office - CRO) were two books of overseers' accounts, one covering the period 1714-1744 and the other 1817-1830.

For the first 10 years of the earlier book, payments ranged from £14 to £28 a year, whereas a century later they ranged from £200 to £360, a tenfold increase. This raised the question as to what caused this increase and whether the underlying changes in the village structure were similar to those occurring elsewhere. Some were taught in their school days that rural deprivation was due to the enclosure of the open fields. As Quy was not enclosed until 1839, it could not have been a relevant factor in this study.

Between 1714 and 1830 Quy had changed from a largely peasant community to a money based one where the labourers depended for their livelihood on a few large farmers. The population had doubled, the price of commodities had doubled but the amount paid out in what would now be called welfare benefits had increased tenfold. Comparison with national and county figures shows that this was not abnormal. As Quy is a small village it is possible to study it in depth but the findings are relevant to many other communities.

This is the second in a series of monographs produced by the Staine Hundred Local History Society. "Bottisham Enclosed - 1801" by Hugh Rogers was partly based on work by James Fitch written as a dissertation for the Certificate of Local History in 1976. My dissertation submitted at that time has been extended and rewritten to form the present publication. I am most grateful to Hugh Rogers for all his help and constructive criticisms.

1 GENERAL DESCRIPTION

THE VILLAGE

Quy is a small village, five miles east of Cambridge. The name means "cow island", its boundaries being streams or fen, except for the relatively high ground (60-70 ft.A.S.L.) along the road to Little Wilbraham to which it was once joined in the south-east (RCHM 1972). It is one of a string of fen edge villages that linked Cambridge to the ancient port of Reach.

There were originally two settlements, Stow and Quy, but these were treated as one village as early as Domesday Book. Although the official name remains as Stow cum Quy, it has always been known locally as Quy, and the shorter name will be used here. Ecclesiastically the parishes were joined in 1289 and the present church was rebuilt on the site of the Stow church in 1340. By the 18th century it stood isolated from the village. Stow remained a separate group of houses to the west of Quy where the houses clustered round the crossroads and the village street leading to Quy Hall. (See map on page 3)

During the 18th century there was no growth - the 1674 Hearth Tax records 40 houses, and in 1794 Vancouver stated there were 36 houses and 39 families. Quy Hall and most of the village had been acquired by the banking family of Martin in the mid 1720s and remained in their hands until 1854.

THE TURNPIKE ROAD

In 1745, the Paper Mills Trust laid out the Turnpike Road from the Paper Mills (behind the Globe Inn) on the outskirts of Cambridge to Newmarket Heath where it joined what later became the A11. The Turnpike cut through the open fields between Quy Water and Quy Church, then eastwards along the line of a track between furlongs for about a mile before once more cutting through open fields on its way to Bottisham (see map). It by-passed Quy so probably had very little impact on village life.

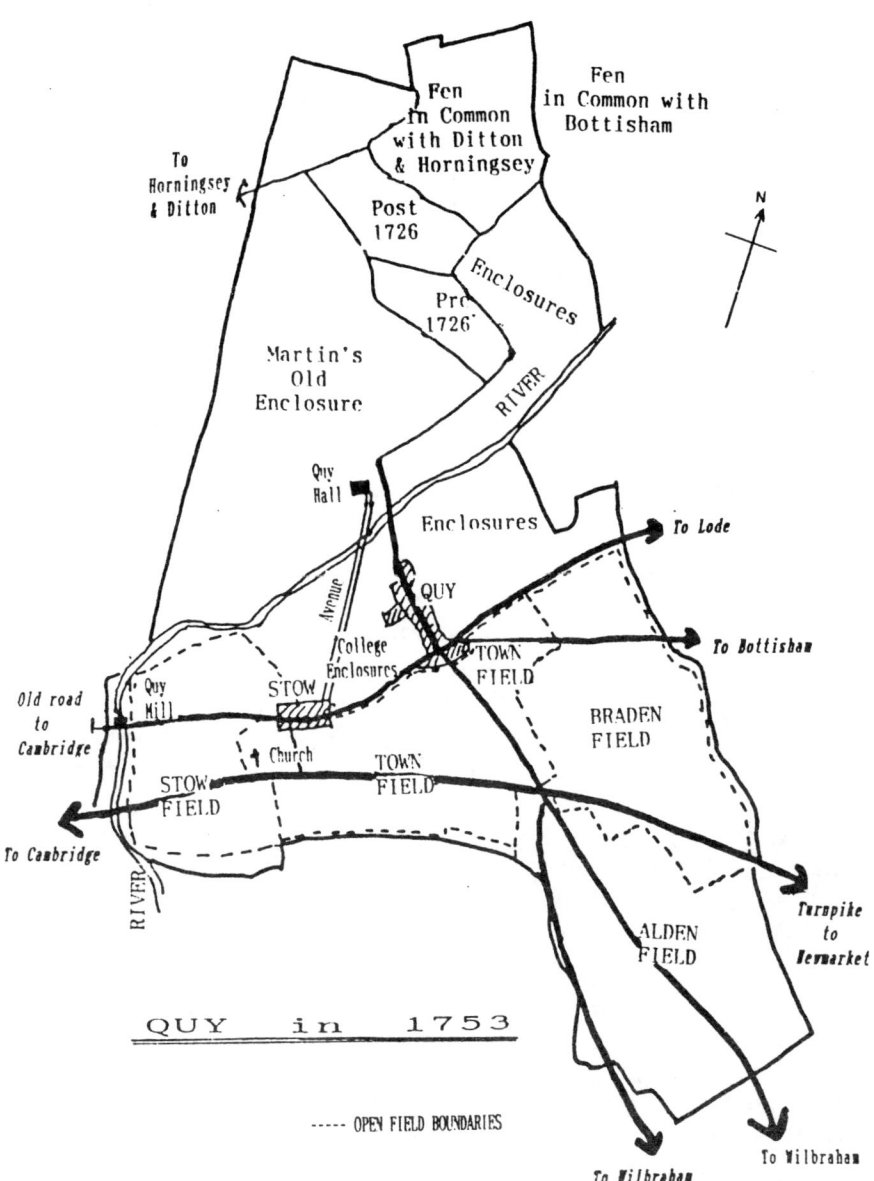

FIELD SYSTEM

Quy covered an area of 1820 acres: to the south were the open fields and to the north the land already enclosed and the common fen.

Open Fields

There were four open fields: Alder, Town (or Home), Stow and Braden - the latter two being regarded as one for the three year rotation of crops. According to Vancouver (1794) there were 1000 acres in the open fields and the rent charged in 1794 was 10s.6d. per acre in Quy as compared with 9s.6d. in Bottisham and 10s. in Little Wilbraham. Yet presumably it was not better land since wheat, barley and peas gave higher yields per acre in Bottisham than Quy, though Quy grew better oats. Since Martin owned or leased most of the land, he was able to let whole furlongs which could be cropped as one field which probably commanded higher rents. A 1778 lease (CRO) shows Newman had several complete furlongs in his 60 acres in each of the three fields on which he was required to keep a three-year rotation.

The Enclosures

The enclosures to the north and west of Quy Hall mostly belonged to the Martins, including one called the "Plowland in the Sheepwalk" which shows that some sheepwalk had disappeared before 1726.(CRO R52.6.1-14).

What is now Quy Park was not part of the Quy Hall estate until after the 1839 enclosure. In Saxon times it was owned by Edeva; it passed to Grimbald the Goldsmith at the time of the Norman Conquest; then became Brians Manor in the 13th and 14th centuries. Much of it became the property of Anglesey Abbey and passed to various Cambridge Colleges after the Reformation. Martin leased it from them.

By 1726 there were seven enclosures of the fen edge, each with a non-Quy owner. By the time the 1753 estate map (now in the CRO) was drawn there were a further seven enclosures, each of 7 acres, but the Martins owned five of these, as opposed to only one of the earlier ones. Perhaps the Lord of the Manor instigated these enclosures to ensure there was no further infiltration by neighbouring parishes?

The Common Fen

The fens in the north east of the village were held in common with adjoining villages: 40 acres with Bottisham and 69 with Ditton and Horningsea. This latter fen was known as 100 Acres but, as mentioned above, had gradually been whittled away by enclosure as the fens became better drained. Hayward's "Original Survey of the Fens 1656" suggests a much larger common fen than existed in the 18th century. In 1720 there was a Memorandum entered in the Overseers' Book but the page is unfortunately damaged at the edges.

> **Memorandum** It is agreed by & between . . . .
> Stow cum Quy that No Poor Man or W . . . .
> keep or lend any Cows in the Comon Fe. . . . . . .
> Meadow nor shall any Farmer or owner F . . . . . .
> or stake more than three Horses or Mares to one. .
> one time: And further it is also agreed that the
> Comin Platt & Comon Fen Shall be Fed by no Farmers
> Cattle the Same shall be Wholly and Solly to the
> use of the Poor and no other Person or Persons
> whatsoever   Witness our Hands...

There were 14 witnesses to this Memorandum which suggests some general meeting had been called. Of these six could sign their name and eight signed with a mark, so it is likely that the farmers and the "Poor" had been present.

It would appear that the farmers were being stinted on the common fields or pasture which lay between the open fields and the boundary ditches and excluded from the Common Fen, whereas the Poor had no rights of common except in the Fen. Presumably the poor were at that time allowed to graze their animals in the Fen but by the beginning of the 19th century no animals were allowed in the fen with the possible exception of a horse or donkey tethered while its owner cut or gathered hay. The poor were allowed to dig turf in the fen.

2 POPULATION AND FAMILY SIZE

POPULATION

A population trend may be obtained by comparing the number of births and deaths recorded in the Parish Registers.

Table 1

	Births	Deaths	Change per decade
1701-1750	342	372	-6.0%
1751-1800	410	257	+30.6%
1801-1830	418	182	+78.3%

Table 1 shows that births and deaths were almost equal in the first half of the 18th century but that in the second half, and even more at the beginning of the 19th century, the difference between them grew as the number of births increased while the number of deaths decreased. This must have led to an increase in population. The same pattern is reported nationally (Mitchell 1962): little growth 1701-1750; a 50% increase from 6m to 9m 1751-1800; and then doubling from 9m to 18m by 1851.

The Census figures for the first half of the 19th century show that Quy was not typical of the County as a whole. In 1801-1810, the County of Cambridgeshire increased by 12,000 and then by 20,000 for each of the next four decades. Quy increased by 75, from 235 to 310, in the first decade and then the increases steadily fell (68,22,45,10) to reach a population of 455 in 1851 - about the same figure as it is now in the 1990s. Quy grew more rapidly during the early part of the 19th century than the other villages in the Staine Hundred (see Fig.1). Cambridge grew most rapidly in the 1820s from 14,000 to 21,000, as the results of enclosing the land surrounding the town began to take effect and more land became available for housing (Taylor,1973). This may have had repercussions on the villages in close proximity to the town. It was not a prosperous time for agriculture and the new development must have created jobs for building labourers and carpenters.

- 6 -

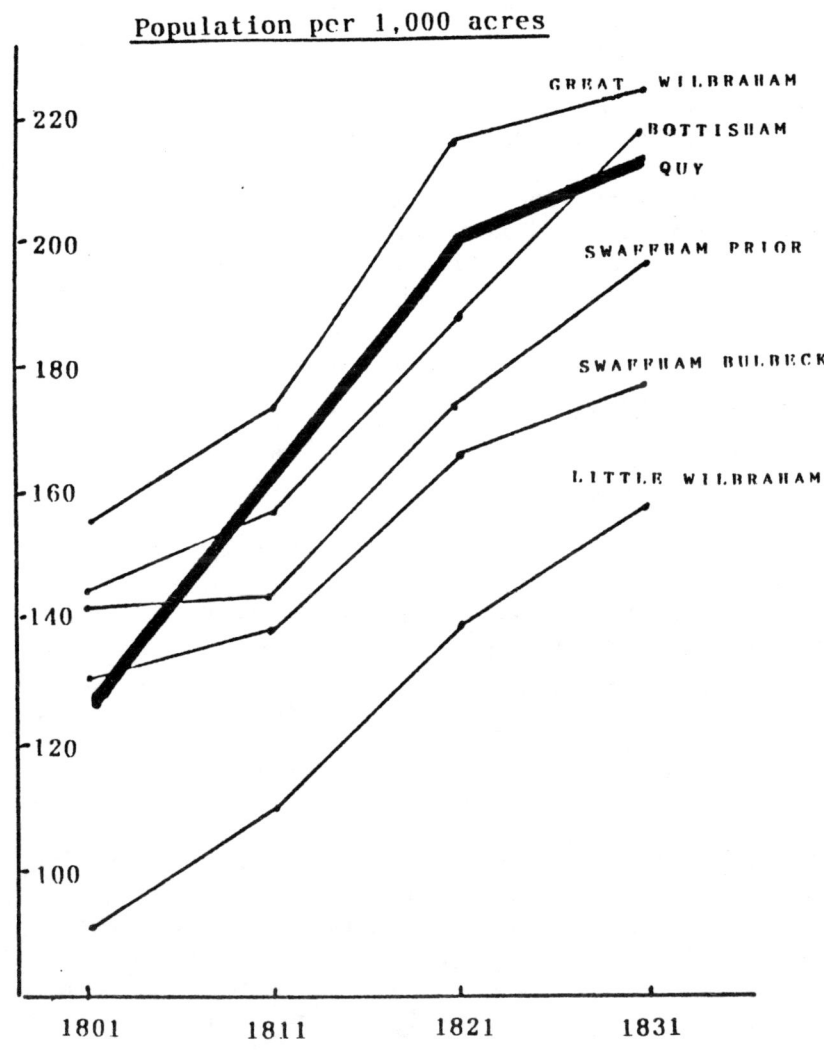

Fig. 1

Thus the first set of Overseers Accounts (1714-1744) concern a period of population stability but the second set begin at a time when very rapid expansion was beginning to slow down yet housing in the village had not kept pace adequately with the increased population. The number of houses reported in the Census returns were 53 in 1811, 69 in 1821 but only 62 in 1831. Some of the earlier increase may have been achieved by subdividing existing houses which perhaps reverted to single houses again as family size grew. In 1825 the overseer entered "Journey to Bottisham by order of Mr Jennings respecting John Muggleton and Edward Ison having a better house to live in when he was satisfied of what I had done". The fact that an appeal was made to Mr Jenyns of Bottisham Hall as JP, even if unsuccessful, would seem to suggest that the housing was not entirely satisfactory.

MARRIAGE PATTERNS

Changes in population growth are likely to cause, or be caused by, changes in the general marriage pattern: the age at which marriage took place, duration of the marriage, number of children, infant mortality etc. Although information obtained by reconstructing families from the Parish Registers is incomplete, it does show some interesting trends.

AGE AT FIRST MARRIAGE

In the early 18th century men tended to marry three years later than their female counterparts (25.6-22.3 yrs). A century later the men were slightly younger when they married, generally being between 21 and 26 (Av=24.7) and the women tended to be four years younger mostly between 17 and 22 but their average age is raised to 23.3 by a number of single women who married widowers when in their 30s and 40s. Probably these older women had been away in domestic service but welcomed the chance to settle down in the village in homes of their own.

LENGTH OF MARRIAGE

In the early 18th century, two-thirds of marriages ended because the wife died and the average length of marriage was only 12 years. John Muggleton was an exception: he enjoyed 45 years of marriage and, according to his inventory he was comfortably off, living in a house with 11 rooms and farming a medium size farm. After his first wife died, he married again in 1713 - this time to a lady from Kent (age unknown) and the marriage ended with his death 17 months later.

By the 19th century, the wife had an almost equal chance of outliving her husband and marriages lasted longer. At least half the married couples reached their silver wedding and five (7%) reached their golden weddings.

CHILDREN

It is natural that the longer marriages and better survival rate of the women should result in larger families being born in the 19th century. The average number of children rose from 4.1 to 6.4. In the early 18th century only 4% of the families had more than 7 children whereas 100 years later 40% had families of this size. The infant mortality rate dropped by almost half from 32% to 17% in 100 years. It is therefore not surprising that with children between one and ten years there was a slight rise in the death rate from 5% to 8%. Bad home conditions, malnutrition, or lack of medical care were no doubt responsible for many of these deaths but there had been some improvements, particularly in medicine, and babies who earlier would have only lived a few weeks or months managed to struggle for a little longer. Thus in general, about two in three babies born in the early 18th century survived whereas in the early 19th century the survival rate was three out of four.

At a rough estimate a child was born every 18 months during the reproductive period of the marriage in the 18th century and every 17 months in the 19th century. Thus conception rate was probably very similar but the factors mentioned above which decreased infant mortality may have had the same effect on the number of miscarriages and still births of which there is no record.

3 SQUIRE AND VICAR

SQUIRE

When the 18th century accounts began, Sir Paul Whichcote was the Lord of the Manor and a JP, living at Quy Hall. He signed the Overseers' Accounts in 1716 and 1717 but he died in 1721. His son, Sir Francis Whichcote, went to St. Catherine's College in 1708 at the age of 16, to Trinity Hall in 1711 and to the Inner Temple in 1714 (Sedgwick 1970). In 1718, when one of the Cambridge members of Parliament died, Sir Francis put up as MP in his place and was returned unopposed. However at the general election in 1722 he lost his seat and did not stand for Parliament again. Shortly after this he sold the Quy estate to the Martin family.

William Martin lived here for a few years but after his death the estate passed to his son Thomas who in 1726, sold the estate to his brother James for £11,500 (CRO 52.6.1-14). About a year later James became senior partner of the bank in Lombard Street, London, so the estate was leased out until his retirement in 1741 when he came to Quy to live. He too was then returned unopposed as MP for Cambridge. Unfortunately "he was much afflicted with the stone, which brought him to the grave in the middle of life" aged 50 in 1744.

After that Quy Hall was once again let to a number of wealthy gentlemen probably until 1819 when Thomas Martin (nephew of James) retired to the village. As a young man, Thomas had a son by Arabella whom he subsequently married. This illegitimate son bore his father's name but was not allowed to inherit. He became a Captain of the 14th Regiment of Native Infantry in the East Indian Company of Bengal until he lost his eyesight in a battle in the East Indies. Thomas and Arabella subsequently had two daughters. The heir to the estate came from Thomas's second marriage - to Ann, a lady younger than his own daughters. When Thomas died in 1821, James was only 15 years old, and he did not take up a permanent residence at Quy Hall until after his marriage. Thus the Squire was largely an absentee one.

THE VICAR

Whereas a resident Vicar could perhaps have filled the gap left by an absentee squire, there had been no resident Vicar in Quy since the death of Stephen Rant in 1681. Quy was relatively accessible from Cambridge and the incumbency was filled by a succession of young men from one or other of the Cambridge Colleges who continued to live and study in Cambridge. One of these short incumbencies, from 1719-1721, was held by Thomas Herring who went on to become first Archbishop of York and then Archbishop ofCanterbury. (The first Council estate in Quy was called Herring's Close as it was completed in 1958 exactly 200 years after his death.)

Thomas Harrison, Regius Professor of Hebrew and a Fellow of Trinity College, held the living from 1743 to 1753 when he died of smallpox at the age of 36. The Latin inscription on the tomb erected in Quy churchyard by his mother described him as "a learned man, excellent, pious and distinguished in the conduct of his life, of outstanding abilities, cultivated in learning, trained in all virtue which grace a man or exalt a Christian" (Cambs Family History Society 1985). There are very few deaths in that year in Quy so it seems unlikely that he caught smallpox when executing his parish duties.

This succession of Cambridge clergy ended in 1784 when the Rev. James Hicks, squire of Great Wilbraham, rector of Wistow in Hunts, magistrate of the County, Chairman of the Quarter Sessions, became the incumbent of Quy - a post he held for 40 years. He used to drive over to Quy on a Sunday afternoon in an open phaeton with yellow wheels, drawn by a pair of grey horses and with a postilion in sky blue livery to look after the horses while he was in church (King,1934). He was succeeded by Rev. Edward Ventris who was Vicar of Quy for 61 years. It was said that he walked from Cambridge every Sunday, calling at the Globe for his glass of beer (King,1934). He lived with his family in Bateman Street, was Chaplain of the Gaol and spent much of his time in the University Library. (Cambridge Chronicle 24.9.1886).

For the ordinary village folk, the Vicar must have been as inaccessible as the Squire.

4 LANDOWNERS

By the middle of the 18th century, most of the land was under the control of the Lord of the Manor, either by ownership or by leasing from Cambridge Colleges (CRO Leases and Land Tax Returns, Magdalen College). As the owners of even small pieces of land had a certain amount of independence, it is important to see whether their number was increasing or decreasing.

The 1757 and 1825 Land Assessments are summarised in Table 2. The units are £1 rateable value which is not the same as acreages, since arable land would have been more highly valued than some of the marginal fenland. Cambridge College land is probably underestimated in both Returns as when it was leased to other landowners it was sometimes included in their total. Table 2 shows that the number of landowners had decreased by 1825.

Table 2

Landowners - Tax Assessments of 1757 & 1825

1757	UNIT	%	1825	UNIT	%
MARTIN, J.	498½	66%	MARTIN, T.	547	72%
FARROW F.	93	12%	AMBROSE W.C.	117	16%
HALFEHIDE Mrs	54	7%			
SERICOLD Mr	27½	3½%			
ALLING, R	17)				
CULLEDGE, R	11)				
MUGGLETON, H	10)	6%	CAIUS COLL.	50)	
RYCROFT, Mr	6)		JESUS COLL.	9)	
BENNET COLL.	21	3%	BENNET COLL.	18)	10%
Three Units or less			Three Units or less		
7 Quy owners	12)		3 Quy Owners	4)	
5 Non-Quy	9)	3%	4 Non-Quy	9)	2%

Francis Farrow who owned 12% of the land in 1757 died and his widow married George Banks. The inventory of his goods at the time of his death in 1759 shows a value of £259.12.3 and that he lived in a house with three chambers, parlour, hall, kitchen, a "strong beer cellar" and a "small beer cellar" and a dairy. This is believed to be the Old Farmhouse opposite the Wheatsheaf. It was later acquired by William Cole, who left it to his grandson William Cole Ambrose, who by 1825 was paying tax on 16% of the land in Quy

Overall the number of landowners in Table 2 had dropped from 21 (759 units) to 12 (754 units) as the two larger landowners, Martin and Ambrose, extended their holdings. The number of small landowners with less than three units fell from 12 in 1757 to 7 in 1825, and it may well have already decreased in the early part of the 18th century. In 1825, the seven small landowners included four non-residents (Lord Aylesford, Cotton, Jenyns of Bottisham and Trig Collier who farmed mainly in Horningsea and two Quy residents who had acquired their land from non-residents (John Flack from his Bottisham father-in-law and Robert Randall from two different owners). One can only conjecture as to whether village people were pressurised to give up their small fen enclosures to the absentee banker Lord of the Manor while the outsiders were more independent of him.

The pattern of land ownership in the early 19th century can be contrasted with that in two neighbouring parishes (CRO 334/045,1825). In Bottisham (which at that time included Lode), much more land was owned (or controlled) by the Cambridge Colleges - 32% and a further 6% owned by Bartholomews Hospital. At Little Wilbraham as in Quy, the Colleges owned about 10% of the land. At Little Wilbraham, there was no very large estate but two people owned approximately 15% each and three others had between 5% and 10% each. The most significant difference however was in the number of small owners. In Quy there were only 7, who collectively held 2% of the land; in Little Wilbraham 17 owners for 37% of the land; but in Bottisham there were 84 owners for 39% of the village.

Martin owned 72% of the land in Quy but it was all let. Although Jenyns owned only 29% of Bottisham he did farm the land himself, and as Bottisham is more than three times the acreage of Quy he was in fact the bigger of the two landowners and was a much more influential figure locally. Accounts to be signed or disputes to be settled at Quy were usually taken to Jenyns of Bottisham as the local JP in both the 18th and 19th centuries.

5 18th C. PARISH OFFICERS

The elected parish officers were all-important in the running of the village, particularly in the virtual absence of both squire and vicar. Churchwardens. overseers, surveyors, and constables were elected annually at the Vestry Meeting. A study of who filled these posts reveals also something of the social and agricultural structure in force at that time.

The number of overseers nominated as eligible varied from two to six. From these two were chosen, each of whom kept the accounts and made the disbursements for six months. In the 30 years 1716-1745, a total of 26 people were reckoned to be eligible though only seven were nominated five or more times, which suggests there was no shortage of choice for the task.

Table 3

Overseer	Dates	Eligible	Served
MUGGLETON, Thomas	1728-44	13	10
WEBB, Richard	1720-33	8	7
FARROW, John Jun.	1735-45	8	8
FARROW, John Sen.	1722-29	6	3
HOVILL, William	1716-32	7	5
CURTIS, Robert	1716-43	7	5
FOOTE, Richard	1719-28	5	3

Thomas Muggleton, who died in 1714, was the grandson of John Muggleton, mentioned earlier as having a very long marriage. Twelve years later, in 1726, when his son Henry died, the value of the farm goods (stock, implements and crops) had increased from £61 to £434. and another two rooms had been added to the house. Thomas, the only one of Henry's three sons to survive, must have been one of the biggest farmers in Quy. He first served as Overseer at the age of 28 and died at the age of 74, outliving both his sons. The 1726 Martin lease shows that Henry Muggleton leased a farm house with all the outbuildings, including dovehouses, a cottage, another tenement with yards and outhouses, a number of closes, fenland and arable land, including some land in Bottisham. He also had a sheep walk and the liberty to fold sheep in the common fields and a sheep pen at Dunsey Cross (now the Prince Albert). He rented 40 acres of arable called Bryans, and had liberty of fold, course and sheepgate, belonging to a messuage called Bryans. This latter land belonged to Bennet College (Corpus Christi) who had leased it to Sir Roger Jenyns of Ely in 1714 for 21 years for £12.10s. per year. Jenyns transferred the remainder of the lease to Martin in 1726. It seems probably that the farm was in the middle of what is now Quy Park.

Richard Webb lived in the "Farm House standing near Holme Hall (old name for Quy Hall) with the farm and lands, all and every barne, stable, coach house, outhouse, dovehouse, folds, yards, orchard and garden and all those closes or parcels of land lying north of the river." There followed a list of 21 closes covering 334 acres. Again he was one of the more prosperous farmers.

There are Farrows recorded in the Quy Registers from 1636 onwards, though it is difficult to reconstruct a family tree and strangely the name does not appear in the Hearth Tax Returns (1662-1674). John Farrow, senior, died in 1731 and his son John was first responsible for the accounts in 1735. In 1736, it was decided that "The Widow Farrow or son" should be overseer, and apparently left for them to sort out who did the accounts. John Farrow seems to have kept the book but at the end of the year they are called "Wedd. Farrow Disburstments" so perhaps it was a joint effort. Her son acted as an overseer at least 8 times. Though it was unusual for a woman to be considered fit to serve as an overseer, Widow Farrow was again nominated in 1739. As already mentioned, the Farrows had a large farm at the Stow End of the village (p.12).

The Hovills were also a long-standing family, the birth and death of a daughter appearing in the first surviving register in 1599. They must have owned their own house as in 1726 they were only renting from Martin three small closes, 22 acres of pasture in High Fen and 14 acres of arable dispersed in the common fields. John Hovill was overseer in 1717 and 1719, on the first occasion jointly with his son William who later did several spells of duty. John died in 1720 and William in 1732 leaving his widow with four stepsons and one son, ranging in age from 1 to 9 years.

Alice Curtis, widow, was buried on October 4th 1727, though her inventory is dated July 4th 1728! She had a house with 9 rooms, four horses, eight cows, three pigs, two carts, two ploughs and three harrows. The farm may have been run by her son Robert though they did not rent land from Martin in 1726.

Richard Foote was another Overseer who did not rent from Martin and little is known of him. Although he was five times eligible as overseer, his stay in Quy may have been relatively short. The family appear in the Registers only between 1719 and 1731, during which time he had seven children of whom only two survived.

Of the other 18 reckoned to be eligible, only three never actually served. These included James Martin, the squire, nominated in 1739 and 1740 after his retirement from the bank; John Raby, a small holder who in 1724 was paid 1s. by the overseers for "going to plow"; and Lawrence Ostler who rented a cottage, yard and croft in 1726 and who probably combined a trade with his small scale farming as he was paid 6s.6d. for a pauper's coffin in 1723 and 1s. "for work and nails" in 1725.

At least four of those who did serve as overseers signed other documents with their "mark", including William Hovill, John Hovill, John Taylor and Richard Howlett. Did their wives keep their accounts for them? Nevertheless twice as many small farmers as large farmers were considered to be eligible to serve as overseer by the standards of their day.

James Moore and John Bett in the 1740s are the only known surveyors. The Parish Clerk was a permanent post and he received payments from the overseers for ringing the bell and digging the grave for pauper funerals. Adam Pur who was Parish Clerk at the time of his death in 1795 could not sign his name, but presumably Richard Piper (d.1726) could as in "Mch 1725 Paid Goodman Piper his fees for marrying of John Sewell 2s 6d"

6   19th C. PARISH OFFICERS

By the 19th century the running of the village had passed into the hands of six farmers. who between them acted as overseers, surveyors and churchwardens and thus set both Poor Rates and Church Rates. In the period 1818-1829 from four to seven overseers were nominated from which one was chosen to keep the accounts.

Table 4

Overseer	Date	Eligible	Served	Rentals
DOBSON, Joseph	1818-29	12	4	192
PRINCE, John	1818-29	12	2	133
ELLIS, John	1818-29	12	2	133
PAYNE, John A.	1821-29	9	1	142
AMBROSE, William	1825-29	5	2	118
COLLETT, J.	1819-25	7	0	25

<u>Joseph Dobson</u> lived in Brown's Park in what is now Quy Park. This was the largest farm as judged by rentals or units in the Land Tax Returns as can be seen in Table 4. He had six daughters (born 1818-1827) but no sons. As well as being overseer he was surveyor for the village roads from 1820-1828, constable in 1818 and churchwarden eight times between 1819 and 1829. Perhaps he spent too much time on public duties instead of on his farm as he went bankrupt in 1838 and died two years later at the age of 51. Joseph was the third son of George and Dinah Dobson and had lived in Quy all his life. His father ran Hall Farm from the time of his marriage in 1785 to his death in 1818. The following four years, his widow Dinah was nominated and served for one year as overseer in 1821, after which she gave up the farm. Dr. Burn (1814) wrote in a book intended to give legal interpretations of the Poor Law Acts to overseers, "where there are a sufficient number of men qualified to serve they are certainly more proper" and that JPs were unlikely to approve the appointment of a woman "when there are other proper objects". It is known that Pauls of Bottisham had a copy of this book which was well-used. Dinah Dobson's appointment was therefore unusual. She tended to give more detail in the accounts than the men and it is clear that she was undertaking the full duties including visits to solicitors.

22.4.1822   Journey to Bottisham after Mr Ambrose Rate when Mr Jenyns directed me to apply to Mr Pemberton
6.5.1822   Journey to Bottisham after Mr Ambrose Rate when I was order to meet the Justices of the County Gaol to hear Mr Ambrose defence
9.5.1822   Journey to Cambridge to meet Mr Ambrose when he promised to pay the rate if the Sheriff did not and Mr Hicks promised to call upon the Undersheriff on the business.

There had been a two day sale of all of Richard Ambrose's farming stock and household furniture the previous December while he was managing the farm for his under-age son. Fifty rentals of land rented to Ambrose by Caius College were transferred to Dobson about this time, and a new tenant was also found for the 14 acres of charity land. It seems clear he was in financial difficulty, so it is not surprising that although he was three times qualified to serve as overseer he was not called upon to keep the accounts. Family sources suggest that he was not trusted by his father-in-law William Cole who left the farm to his grandson, William Cole Ambrose. The latter first kept the overseer's accounts in 1825 at the age of 22 and became one of the stalwart figures of Quy (Watts,1993).

The farmhouse (opposite the Wheatsheaf) where the Ambrose family lived. The big barn disappeared in the 1930s.

John Ellis of Park Farm was an assessor for the Land Tax Returns. He was a member of the Swaffham Bulbeck farming family and his children do not appear in the Quy registers. The Ellis family continued at Park Farm until 1911.

John Prince had been farming at Quy since the beginning of the century, possibly in a farm in Orchard Street. He was an assessor of the Land Tax as well as churchwarden and constable continuously for the period of the overseers' accounts 1818-1829. He was left a widower with five children under 10 years in 1814 and two of these children died during the 1820s. As he did not remarry, perhaps his home comforts were not ideal and this may have made him more willing to take on parish duties.

John Augustus Payne was a relative of Thomas Martin. In 1819 when Martin retired to Quy Hall at the age of 70 he was made overseer. He kept the accounts for about a fortnight and then handed them over to Payne who signed and verified them on oath as "Deputy Overseer of the Poor for Thomas Martin Esq.". John Payne was probably staying at Quy Hall but he could have known little of the village - or indeed about the overseer's duties. Perhaps this led him to consult John Prince who was well versed in such tasks as the following year, Payne married Prince's eldest daughter. When Mrs Dobson sold up a little later, he took over the Hall Farm. From then on he was regularly nominated as overseer and was twice churchwarden.

Although John Collett and his son John who succeeded him had only a modest sized farm, he also had a successful milling business at Quy Mill. They were considered to be eligible as overseers but never kept the accounts. It could be that millers were busier than other farmers during the winter months when there was most call on their services, or that Quy Mill was too remote.

The blacksmith, John Flack, who owned property, was constable throughout this time but was never considered as an overseer - though it seems likely that he would have been deemed so a century earlier.

WIDOWS

One of the main tasks of the overseers was to maintain those in need, of whom the widows were an important group.

18th CENTURY WIDOWS

During the period of the accounts, 1714-1744, at least 38 widows lived for some or all of their widowhood in Quy, but half of them received no regular payments from the overseers, though some had their rents paid from time to time. Since death in, or as a result of, childbirth was common, there would have been fewer women than men in the community over the age of about 25. Widowers left with small children would have been glad to take on a widow to look after the house and children on a temporary basis in exchange for their upkeep.

Others were able to continue with their husband's smallholding. For instance:

Pd. Wid Howlett for two tymes going to Stetchworth with her horse and man	3s. 0d.
now for her horse one shilling and my boy 6d	1s. 6d.
Paid for a pound of pork to Widdow Adams for Rob Tomson	1s. 4d.
Leddy Edwards an acre of grass	£1. 2s. 6d.

There are numerous occasions when the overseers paid widows for "the laying in" of some poor woman,"nursing the sick" or "doing for" someone infirm, or "laying out" some pauper. When those requiring such services were already on a subsistence allowance and had no resources to pay for help, the overseer would often call on the help of one of the widows and pay them either in cash or in goods, e.g. "Laying John Asplin out Victuals and drinks 4s."

There must have been many other occasions when widows were asked to undertake such tasks by those who were not destitute, and could perhaps give a bag of flour or a leg of pork as money was less important in a peasant society.

Eight of the widows had regular payments, from 6d. to 2s. a week, as they became old and infirm but none were paid continuously for more than seven years. Some had regular payments for a few years in the middle of their widowhood. The overseer paid the rent of Widow Reeve (or Reed) for three years after her husband died at the age of 24 in 1719 leaving her with two children. Then her mother-in-law died in 1721 so perhaps she kept house for her father-in-law and she received no payments until 1728 when she had regular payments for about a year until her children were apprenticed by the overseers.

Spinning was still a cottage industry and some of the widows may have already been engaged in it. New wheels and wool were occasionally bought for widows to help them be self-sufficient.

7.10.1720	A new wheel for the Widow Newman	2s. 6d.
21.3.1725	For a new weel for the widdow Thomson	1s. 6d.
29.9.1737	A spinning weel to Wid Bridgman	1s. 6d.
5.3.1738	The Wedd Dossiter 1 pound wool	1s. 3d.

At that time it was compulsory for people to be buried in wool and the paupers' funerals sometimes show an entry for wool and an affidavit to prove that it had been done.

11.1.1723 Pd. Wid Clarke for laying out of her boy (Numan's son) 6d.
& fer a coffin to Lawrence Oslar 6s. 6d.
& to Piper to burying charges 2s. 6d.
& fer an affidavit 6d.

John Edwards died in 1728. His first wife had died soon after giving birth to her third child who only lived a few months. John soon married again to Elizabeth Noble by whom he had another six children, of whom half died very young. After John's death Elizabeth received about 20 payments of various amounts. In 1729, Elizabeth's step daughter died aged 29. A month later, the overseer paid 3d "for a dose of batmans drops" for Widow Edwards but they could not have been very effective:

15.5.1730	Widow Edwards for to go to the doctor	2s. 0d.
	Paid for hir shift	2s. 6d.
2.10.1730	Paid for a coffin for Widow Edwards	7s. 0d.
	Paid the clerk	2s. 6d.
	Laying hir out and wool and vitels for the women	3s. 0d.
	Carrying her to be buried and spent	1s. 6d.

There are many entries of turf being supplied to the poor, and widows could not be expected to cut their own turf from Quy Fen. Often 1,000 turves would be delivered to one person at a time. Some of it was bought outside the village:

23.9.1720	For 8000 of turf and fetching them to Quy	£2. 0s. 0d.
4,10,1728	The poores firing 14 thousan	£4.11s. 0d.
	for carting them in	9s. 9d.
29.9.1731	Paid Rich<u>d</u> Smith for 18 thousan and five hundred of turfe for the poor	£2. 6s. 0d.
	For caring the poors firing from Bottisham	£1. 1s. 0d.

Thus it would seem that unless widows were ill or infirm they managed to survive with support from the local community without having to ask for regular payments

19th CENTURY WIDOWS

By the early 19th century, times had changed. The gap between rich and poor had widened. There is no evidence of any spinning and there was little chance of the widows picking up the odd job from their neighbours. The overseers still paid them for helping out at times of birth, death or illness but in general as soon as a husband died, his widow had to live "on the parish".

Between 1817 and 1830, sixteen widows are known to have lived at Quy. Four were widows of farmers or businessmen who carried on their trade, such as John Prince's sister Mrs Kerridge who continued to keep the Cock Inn and run her late husband's blacksmith's business. The other 12 received weekly payments from the time of their husband's death till their own death (9), or remarriage (2), unknown (1). For instance George Chapman died suddenly in 1825, the circumstances are not known but the overseer paid 7s. expenses for the Coroner's inquest. His widow immediately received 2s a week which was raised to 2s. 6d. in 1828, and continued thus to the end of the accounts. She had three married daughters and one married son living in Quy, and one unmarried son in his twenties who may have left the village, so there does not seem to have been any pressure to make them responsible for their mother as happened a century later. Usually there were six and eight widows on the overseer's book at any one time, and the standard payment was 2s. per week.

8 ORPHANS & FATHERLESS

Although widows seemed to get more help from the overseers in the 19th century than in the earlier period, the opposite was true of the orphans and fatherless children. In both sets of accounts there are children supported by the parish who had one parent living.

18th CENTURY CHILDREN

Hampson (1934) wrote that before the middle of the 18th century "a system of placing out pauper children for a few months at a time with the inhabitants had developed in many rural parishes". Henry Smith was one such boy. He was the son of Thomas and Mary Smith and baptised at Quy in May 1721, though his parents were not married here. Thomas does not seem to be directly descended from the other Smiths in the village, and whether he died or left his wife is not known. The overseers paid several months lodging "for Thomas Smiths wife until she went a waye" in 1722, and presumably she returned to her original parish taking her young son with her. However when Henry was 7 years old he was returned to Quy as the place of his birth and the overseers had to arrange for his upkeep.

At various times Henry Smith lived with Edy Asplen, Widow Numan, and Widow Russell but for most of the time he was boarded with one of the farmers, Robert Curtis, William Hovill or Henry Muggleton. Normally 1s.6d. was paid a week for his keep but this was often reduced to 1s. or 6d in the summer months when he was boarding with a farmer so presumably he partly earned his keep. Between 1725 and 1736, the overseers bought for him 15 pairs of shoes, 18 pairs of hoses or stockings, 14 pairs of breeches, 8 waistcoats, 5 coats, 15 shirts, 4 hats and 1 cap. Sometimes stockings were "home nett", the cloth was bought and the coat made for him, or his clothes or shoes were mended. When he was 14, the overseers charged 5s. for his indentures and their expenses, and 15 months later there were 5s. expenses to bind him out and £3.10s. paid to John Claksen at the same time.

William Mason was a shoemaker but he and his wife often had three or four children living with them who were taught how to spin. In 1730, there is an entry "paid the Widow Adames for a pund of Woll for William Mason for learning of the children to spin". Probably he was able to make some money from the older children's work in addition to the money he was paid for each child's board. One of the children at that time was Elizabeth, daughter of Susan Smith who lodged with him from August 1728 to October 1731 and for whom he was paid 1s.8d per week.

The other three children belonged to John Wibrow. Wibrows had been living in Quy for about a century and were small farmers. John was the youngest of seven and two of his older brothers were still living in Quy with their families, but as the eldest had had eleven children from his two wives, he was probably not a position to help out when John Wibrow's wife died in 1727, leaving John with Prudence aged 7, John 5, and Mary 4. In 1728, John must have gone off and left the children. On May 17th the Overseer paid 2s. for "2 shiftes for John Wybrows children and making" and on May 21st that year there are entries "Paid Mr Yorke for advice and writing concerning John Wybrow 9s." and "Expenses going a bought him 9s.6d." His sister-in-law Mary was paid a total of £3.12.6d for looking after two of his children for 5 months in 1728. These entries were later crossed through as though he had returned and the overseers had been refunded. By April the following year, the overseers were again paying for the upkeep of his three children and the overseer John Briggs and John Farrow spent 2s. when they "went to Bottisham before Sir Roger Jennings concerning John Wibrow." Perhaps as a result of this advice on 11th May 1729 Briggs came to an agreement with William Mason to pay him 5s.6d a week for the three Wybrow children and the Smith girl. Maybe the agreement was made over a glass of beer as the entry ends "and then spent 2s." After two years with William Mason, the children moved to live with their uncle William Wibrow, the two girls being fitted out with "gownds and coates, and lining for the gownd bodys and making" (14s.3d. for the two) and a "pair of lether Boodys for the begest garle" (4s.6d.) and "2 shifts and Apron and making" (4s.). At the end of their six month stay with their uncle, on

13th April 1732, the overseer gave John Wibrow 7s.6d. "upon the account of his promising to release the parish of the charge of his children" and again he spent 2s. at the same time. There is evidence that John Wibrow was a householder in Quy from 1735 onwards. Usually the children became a charge on the parish when the father died and the mother had no money for their upkeep but as Wibrows children had right of settlement because they were born in Quy, the overseers had little option but to take responsibility for them when their father went off.

Both girls and boys were apprenticed by the parish in the 18th century and this could be quite expensive. On the other hand, if they were apprenticed in another town they would gain settlement there and be no further expense to Quy ratepayers. As mentioned in the previous chapter, Widow Reed stopped receiving parish relief once her children had been apprenticed.

	£. s. d.
September 1729	
Paid to Mr Hattley with Elizabeth Reed being the day apprenticed to him	4 4 0.
Now paid to him for her board before she was bound and for things Mr Hattley bought her	1 10 0.
Spent now and several times concerning her	10 6.
Paid now for ye Indentures to Mr Yorke	5 0.
Paid to Mr Cullifer of Cambridge with Francis Reed	10 0.
Spent at several tymes concerning bargaining with Mr Culliver when he took ye said Francis Reed	8 6.
Paid to John Farrow which he had paid before for collecting and offering concerning putting out Wid Reeds children	8 1.
April 1730 Paid to Mr Hattly (2nd half of agreed fee)	4 4 0.

Henry Muggleton, one of the rich farmers in the village was paid £2 for taking an apprentice in 1714 and John Muggleton, a smaller farmer, was paid £2.10s for taking Susan Asplen (an orphan whom the parish had been supporting) in 1715. Her brother's indentures cost 6s.8d. but there is no record of a lump sum. Although 2s.2d. was spent in 1718 "at two Metenes upon binden Ann Ester out prentis" and 3s. in 1735 "spent agoing with Robert Tomson to harren him in his marster horshier" there is no mention of indentures or of lump sums changing hands. These look like cases, to quote Hampson again, where "other methods of placing out children without formal indentures and

- 25 -

for various terms were evolved in the 18th century but in such cases no settlement was acquired." and the overseers often continued to keep them in clothes. There are a number of cases where children were boarded out by the parish for a few years and then still received clothes after their weekly board had stopped.

19th CENTURY CHILDREN

There were four sets of children for whom payments were made when the accounts began in 1817 - in addition to those whose widowed mothers received more than the standard 2s. per week.

Frances Munns was left with four daughters, aged 11, 7, 5 and 2 in 1810 when her husband died. From 1817 to 1821, the overseers paid for the upkeep of the children on a gradually diminishing scale from 6s.6d. down to 1s.6d. as the girls were sent out to service.

"Prestons girl" may not have been living at Quy for much of the time. Her mother was buried at Quy in 1808 but they were not a Quy family. Sometimes her 1s. per week was entered as a lump sum for a whole year and on one such occasion the only other payment on that day was for "the man who came over". Payments ended in November 1823 when 10s. was paid to Elizabeth Preston when she went to service. Probably her father had moved back to his own parish but Elizabeth must have gained Quy settlement.

John Fordham died in 1807 and his widow married again three years later to John Burling. The youngest son David was 10 in 1817 when the accounts began, and it was the overseer's responsibility to pay for his subsistence and not his stepfather. Weekly payments of 1s.6d, later reduced to 1s., stopped when he was 11 or 12 years old.

James Butler who died in 1810 had had two wives, the three surviving children of the first marriage being more or less independent of the parish by 1817, though the youngest girl who went into service at Lode seems to have been ill or out of work in 1819 when the overseer made four payments to her totalling 19s. and kitted her out with clothes and shoes, no doubt to send her off to a new post. The second wife had two boys, John (b.1808) and James (b.1810) for whom the overseers paid 2s.6d. a week until 1819. They were then provided with shoes made by Philip Arber of Bottisham and £3 worth of clothes. Mr Prince (at others times referred to as Dr. Prince or Mr Prince surgeon) was paid 10s. for inoculating them. After that there were occasional entries for "Butlers boy" up to 1824 but these may have been for sickness or unemployment. After the above children became self-supporting, there were no more children for whom the overseers paid weekly, at least up to 1830.

There were a number of other children in the early 19th century who were fitted out when they went into service, sometimes when the father was ill but with others it would seem that although the family could just keep going normally, they had no money for extras. In 1818, William Manning had 8s. when he "whent to servis" at the age of 12 and four years later his sister Dinah at 14 had 6s. "for clothes to go to service with Mr White at Attorney in Cambridge." Their father was sworn in as pindar (whose task was to impound straying cattle) in 1823 and apart from an odd 4s. for a week's illness and 5s. when he had a sore hand he did not need parish relief.

Manning was one of 25 people who received "Childrens Head Money" for his family from April to September 1817. This was a kind of child's allowance which was paid around the end of the Napoleonic Wars when the price of bread rose sky high and the amount paid was related to bread or wheat prices. These payments varied with the number of children and fluctuated between 6d. and 1s.6d for the smallest family and 1s.6d and 4s.6d for the largest family. There is no record of how long they were paid in Quy but in Swaffham Prior, children's pay disappeared by September 1801 but reappeared in April 1812 and continued till August 1817 (Anon, 1955). In much of Cambridgeshire the use of child allowance continued until 1832. There is evidence of children being paid to pick stones from the fields for the upkeep of the roads but most such payments would have been in the surveyors' accounts. There is no mention in the 19th century of apprenticeships involving the overseers in any expense, but there were fewer dependent children than a century earlier.

9   ILLEGITIMACY

18th CENTURY

Between 1715 and 1740, there were only three recorded illegitimate births out of 161 (2%). In two cases the names of both parents were given. Nothing is known about Ann Webb's child. The father of Mary Chivers baby was John Tag and the overseer went to Cambridge to talk to him. A later entry states "Laid out for Mare Chivers for a justes order and expenses 1s.9d." so he must have been ordered to support his child.

Mary Newman had a child by Phillip Challis, a married Quy man who died in 1722 and was given a pauper's funeral. He already had two children so the chances of him contributing towards Mary Newman's child must have been slim, but in any case it only survived him by six months. It was quite customary in those days, if the overseer knew that a girl was expecting an illegitimate baby who could become a burden on the parish rates, to send the girl into a neighbouring parish so that the child born would have settlement in that parish. It seems possible that this may have happened to Mary Newman some eighteen months earlier as on 11 November 1720 the following entries appear in the overseers' book

    Mary Newman for butter and cheese and milk   8d.
    Mary Newman for half a peck of Wheat and a peck of rye   1s. 0d.
    Mary Newman a horse journey over the heath   1s. 0d.

If Mary had been expecting a baby and was taken on horseback "over the heath" in mid winter, the baby's chance of survival would have been slight and the absence of a baptism does not disprove this theory.

There are other entries which show that a pregnant woman from another parish would be given money to move on to the next parish:

        Gave a woman Great with child   1s. 6d.
        To a grated bellied woman   2s. 0d.

19th CENTURY

Between 1816 and 1830, there were eight illegitimate births out of 225 (4%). Samuel Butler's widow whose boys were mentioned in the last chapter, had an illegitimate daughter in 1817. Seven years later she married John Cook, a widower who had been left with ten children and she provided him with two more. His oldest daughter had an illegitimate daughter in 1826. Mary Mallion and Elizabeth Howard had illegitimate children in 1829, but the accounts do not survive much after this so it is not known whether the overseers took any steps to get payment. If the fathers were Quy labourers, it is possible that the overseers could assert enough pressure to get them to pay without taking legal steps. By then the girl could charge a man with being the father and he had to pay.

There was a case reported in the 1830s at Swaffham Prior
"About 8 months ago Maria Benson charged Byford, a waggoner, with being the father of the child she was expecting. Byford immediately left home, and the child was sworn to him. A warrant was taken out for him and when he was traced he was taken back to Swaffham. The girl was then found to be not pregnant, nor ever had been. When asked why she had made such statements, she replied with a simper that she had only done it to get the young man to marry her. Byford was immediately discharged and the girl committed to the Castle to take her trial for wilful and corrupt perjury." (Independent Press).

Perhaps in Quy, someone would have noticed in less than eight months that the girl was not pregnant! But it does show how difficult it was for a man to prove that he was not the father if a girl chose to name him. The overseers were concerned with three cases of illegitimacy. Ann Randall had no Quy settlement and the overseer was anxious that she should not obtain one. In November, six months before the baby was baptised, he went to Wilbraham "to sware Ann Randle to her habitation" and in December he went to Bottisham for the same purpose, presumably to see the magistrates as some legal expenses were involved as well as the journey.

Charlotte Ison was given 3.18s.8d. for her child although it had only lived three months. This was presumably some money that the overseer had extracted from the father.

Mary Unwin had two illegitimate children. The first was born and buried just before the surviving overseers' accounts begin. Before the birth of the second, she was taken before the magistrates to "sware her child" and a warrant was issued "to take the man". They had difficulty in getting Samuel Brooks to pay for the upkeep of his child for any length of time. Warrants were issued in 1818, 1821, 1823 and 1828. Again we can be thankful for Dinah Dobson for giving a little more detail in her entry "Journey to Cambridge to see Samuel Brooks to ask him to pay the money that had been paid by the parish for Mary Unwins child he refused to pay and after that a warrant was granted by the Magistrates to happerhand him"

It would not seem that bastardy was a great problem in Quy. Nor is there any evidence here, as Hampson (1934) suggested that "a rapid increase in immorality and attempts to extort hush money" was becoming fairly frequent. On the other hand, her statement that "during the years of stress and strain in the early 19th century, parish authorities concentrated on the pursuit of such men as it was profitable to catch" would seem to be true at Quy, since apart from the money for Charlotte Ison's child, Samuel Brooks seems to have been the only man the Overseers pursued with any persistency - and even then they had on one occasion to pay 1s. to get him out of prison.

Quy Hall from a photograph taken before 1869. James Martin, when he became an MP in 1741, decided that Quy Hall had no sufficiently imposing apartments in which he could receive his constituents. He rebuilt the two end portions with turrets and gave the whole of the front a coating of white stucco surmounted by a castellated parapet. He also remodelled it by taking out the front middle portion to provide two large rooms both 16 ft. high, hence the small windows above where the rooms were only 4 ft. high!

10   AGED AND   INCAPABLE

"Aged" here refers to the men who had reached the age of 70. Between 1817 and 1830 nine of the nineteen men in this category were completely dependent upon the parish by the time they died.

After farmers were no longer willing to give regular employment to aged men in failing health, the overseers would give them casual work from time to time on the roads or ditches and they probably got some farm work during busy seasons. The job of impounding stray cattle or those put to graze on the common fen was twice given to men over 70; another old man was paid 10s. for "tolling the bell at harvest"; another was given the job of bird scaring and the overseers paid 1s. "to buy powder to keep rooks off the wheat"; Muggleton continued as Parish Clerk well into his 70s. In between such odd jobs, they were able to get some subsistence from the overseer.

When the overseer decided that an old man could no longer work, he was placed on the list of those who received regular weekly payments. The Over 70s accounted for nine of the ten paupers on the disbursements list. The length of time which these nine received weekly sums varied from two to fifteen years. The amount varied, but was generally 3s. for a widower and 5s.6d for a married couple. Two of these paupers were non-resident, perhaps because they had gone to live with one of their married children, but they still had to be supported from Quy rates as that was where they had their settlement.

The ten Over 70s who were not paupers included the Lord of the Manor, one large farmer, two cottage owners, one who "refused to swear he was not without money or cattle and no relief was allowed him so Mr Hicks recommended the Parish Officers to find him work by turns", (which suggests the casual work mentioned above may have been supplied by the overseers on a rota basis). Three of the others had a number of payments for illness and/or parish work. The other was John Newman, a basketmaker who managed to continue with his trade after he was 70. The overseers bought him a bunch of wickers once or twice a year. When he was younger and fitter he presumably went out to the osier holts and cut them for himself. In fact we know that in 1799 he was committed to the Castle for robbing an osier ground belonging to Richard Wheeler. He had cut bundles of green osiers and hid them in the bushes but was caught when he went to collect them after dark (Cambridge Chronicle 31.5.1799).

It would seem that only those with property or a business could be entirely self-supporting in their old age, but the overseers tried to keep the others working as long as possible. The data are too sparse to make a comparison with the 18th century accounts but there were very few who lived to reach the age of 70. One of these was the farmer John Muggleton already mentioned as making a late marriage, another was Thomas Carter who had no parish support, but one cannot be sure if there were any others.

THE INCAPABLE

Three men in the early 18th century accounts needed frequent help from the overseers. Payments were likely to stop and start again whenever a new crisis arose but comparatively more aid was given in goods than cash.

Robert Tompson, a married man with a wife of child-bearing age received financial help at the "laying-in". It seems likely that he was not fit enough to be regularly employed and the overseers paid him a few coppers from 1719 right through to the end of the accounts in 1744. There are a number of payments to women for nursing him, for clothes and for goods, as the following examples show:

A pint of clarret for Tompson	4d.
For 500 turfe	3s. 0d.
Paid to Robt Tomson for beehives	6s. 0d.
Laid out for Robert Tomson and his wife for a bed tiking a pair of sheets two blankets and coverlide	11s. 0d.
Gave Rob Tomson towards an Ass	1s. 0d.
A new shift for his wife	2s. 8d.
Robt Tomsons Rent	8s. 0d.
Paid for a boshel of molt for RT	2s.10d

John Osborn was an old soldier. For much of the time he had 1s.6d a week though this later rose to 2s.6d. In July 1729 the overseer gave him 5s. because he was going to London and he promised it would be his only call on the parish until Michaelmas when they agreed to pay his rent. The following April, the overseer had to reimburse a Mr Gillam who was probably an overseer from another parish with £1.8s.6d. One year, Osborn had 11s.6d. "In Stirbitch time which was designed to buy him some things of Winter". 6d. a week was to be stopped from his allowance until the 11s.6d. was repaid - which seems a very practical idea. In 17 years, John Osborn was provided with 26 shirts, 6 pairs of shoes, 6 pairs of stockings, 2 pairs of britches, 1 coat, 1 sheet, bed and bedding and a pail. Osborn was "very ill" in 1732 and from then until his death in 1743 his leg had to be treated with salve (or "diackolam") for which the overseers paid 5d. a fortnight for ½lb.

John Rant had come down in the world. His grandfather was the last resident vicar (d.1681) until the present vicarage was built in 1884. His father was described as "Gent" in the inventory of his goods after his death. John was married in Sidney Sussex College in 1703 at the age of 32. He had seven children but evidently not the means to maintain them properly at all times. Whether he was ill or farm work was considered unsuitable work for him is not known. In 1720 he received a weekly allowance of 3 pecks of rye and 1 peck of wheat. After that his rent was paid regularly, he had turf with the rest of the poor, his wife was given a pauper funeral, clothes were occasionally bought for his children and he had financial help when he was ill. From 1727 when his wife died he had regular weekly payments but then they stopped in 1734 though no death is recorded (John Rant who died in 1757 could have been him or his son). It is interesting that two of the less literate overseers refer to him as "Mr Rant" though they do not use the title of Mr for anyone else receiving parish relief. Evidently they still acknowledged his "class".

In the 19th century, three single women were invalids and needed continuous support from the overseers. Two were the daughters of widowers who were not working. In addition to weekly payments to pay for subsistence for the pauper and his daughter, neighbours were paid for washing and nursing the invalids. The third lived with her mother and stepfather so separate nursing money was not paid though an allowance was given for the invalid. One died at the age of 30 after a nine-year illness (which may have been consumption) but the other two lived to be 60 and 73.

PAUPER FUNERALS

As mentioned above Rant's wife was given a pauper's funeral. Between 1714 and 1744, expenses for 25 of the 220 funerals (11%) in Quy were paid from the poor rate. In addition the overseers had to pay for two funerals which took place outside the village. These pauper funerals include 14 women (wives and widows), 9 men (mostly aged) and 4 children. If anything, the situation had improved slightly by the early 19th century when 10 of the 130 Quy funerals (8%) plus two external burials (4 women, 6 men and 2 children) had all their funeral expenses paid. However the overseers also paid for the grave-digging for 5 young children and the clerk's expenses for one pauper. In 1826 William Davis of Bottisham was paid £1.2s. for "Palls & Shrouds".

Thus, although by the 19th century the economic plight of many of the labourers had worsened, the percentage of pauper funerals changed little. Funerals had to be paid for in cash and this was less plentiful in earlier times, but later there was probably an instinctive fear of "being buried by the parish" so that people would make sacrifices to put by enough money to pay for their funeral.

11   THE SICK

Inability to earn a living because of an accident or temporary illness is an age-old problem and many instances of payments for these reasons abound in both sets of accounts. Unfortunately the overseers were rarely explicit about the nature of the illness and indeed it is often difficult to know whether illness was the reason for the payment.

SMALLPOX

In the 18th century smallpox was still sufficiently likely to occur in the village for John Arbor to undertake in 1724 to keep Richard Asplen, an orphan "in all sorts of sickness except the smallpox" (Watts, 1977)

> **John Arbor do agree to take Richard Asplen for a year to find him shoes and stockings a shirt and hat and a new pair of breeches to keep him in all sorts of illness except the smallpox**
> **Witness my hand**
> **Richard Foote   (signed) John Arborow**

The burial registers are unhelpful as to the cause of death and the only mention of smallpox here is in 1795 when a 25 year old man, William Morgan, died of the disease. There are however five cases of smallpox mentioned in the overseers accounts between 1714 and 1744. For instance, in 1739 when William Johnson's family suffered from the complaint, the nursing was done by Elizabeth Cocks who had recovered from it nine years earlier. It was probably hard to get anyone willing to care for smallpox sufferers as the overseer paid Elizabeth Cocks 8s. a week which is far higher than a woman would usually expect to earn for nursing

William Johnson Charge when his family had the smallpox	
Apothecarys bill	7s. 6d.
Paid at Wm Hovill for Shop things	6s. 6d.
Money and goods taken at my house	15s. 11d.
To Eliz Cocks Nursing 4 weeks	£1.12s. 0d.
for his lodging and other trouble	4s. 9d.
Beer at Jo Muggletons	2s. 0d.
To half a thousand of turf	2s. 0d.

By the 19th century smallpox vaccination had been shown to be effective. It was proposed in 1823 that a legacy left by John Bowtell to Addenbrooke's Hospital should be spent on building two wings, two stories high, 40 ft x 31 ft, containing four wards, one for surgical, one for vaccination, one for persons labouring under personal deformity and one for convalescents - at a cost not exceeding £3,150. (Cambridge Chronicle). It has already been mentioned that the Butlers children were vaccinated in 1819 by Mr John Prince for 10s.

HOME NURSING

Nursing and midwifery were carried out by local women, often widows. If those requiring attention were unable to pay, then the overseers paid the relevant neighbour for performing the duties which occasionally involved taking the sick person into her house and being paid for board as well as nursing. The nursing pattern changed little in 100 years.

MEDICAL CARE

In the early 18th century medical treatment, for which Quy overseers paid, amounted to only £13.17s.11d. in 30 years and this included the above bill for Johnson and one for John Cocks when they had smallpox. Mr Chapman was paid £3 for curing Ann Asplin's leg when she was at Stetchworth and they also had to pay £1.14s.3d. for her keep while she was there for fifteen weeks. Mr Edward Pratt of Little Wilbraham was paid £1.10s in 1715, and in 1724 he was paid for 1s. for "bleeding the Widow Numan". There were six payments for bleeding and/or purging, eight unspecified cures for the itch; many payments for salve; and others for ointment, physick, mouth water, "botle of water" and "batsmans drops".

A century later the amount paid for medical treatment by the overseers had risen from around 9s. per year to over £9 a year. Thirty five bills amounting to £118.9s.0d. in 13 years were rendered by six doctors, most if not all coming from Cambridge. Mr Wells was most frequently in attendance, and he appears to have been paid £2.10s. as a half-yearly salary, probably to attend the official paupers as one bill is for attendance and extra pauper

10s.6d." The largest single bill was in 1819 for £18.15s.6d. from Dr. Okes, a surgeon living in Trinity Street, Cambridge.

No doubt the old remedies were still being concocted in the village (as indeed they were during the first half of this century) but the overseers no longer paid for them as they had in the past. In 1724 Goody Lawrence was paid 6d. for salve for Su Clarke.

HOSPITAL TREATMENT

Roads had of course vastly improved, particularly with the coming of the Paper Mills Turnpike in 1745. This facilitated not only the doctors coming out from Cambridge but also patients being taken to hospital.

Dr. Addenbrooke who died in 1719 left £4500 in his will for a small physical hospital to be founded (Cooper, 1852). In March 1744, the overseer "Paid for Thomas Numan at the Easpetal 11s.1d." seems to be the only reference to hospital treatment in the existing 18th century accounts.

In the 19th century, the overseers paid a yearly two guinea subscription to Addenbrooke's Hospital, though this is not entered every year in the accounts. In July 1823, Shipp went to hospital with "a sore leg" and the overseer provided him with a new shirt for the occasion (value 2s.8d.) and paid his family 7s. a week for 8 weeks. In October of that year, Edward Mumford was also taken to hospital with a bad leg but was sent home as an outpatient. The annual report of Addenbrooke's Hospital in 1821 stated that many individuals were reluctantly sent home or admitted as outpatients because the hospital was already full. Two or three others who went to hospital are mentioned in the overseers' accounts but there is insufficient detail to know the reason.

Fulbourn Asylum was not built until the middle of the 19th century so when John Muggleton "went out of his mind" he was taken to St. Lukes Hospital in London. For over three weeks he had been supervised night and day in his home in Fen Ditton by one of three Quy men as the Fen Ditton overseers did not accept responsibility for a Quy man. Then these three men accompanied him by coach to London supplied for 16s. by Isaac Marsh, a waggon proprietor in Hobson St, Cambridge. The two overseers travelled more luxuriously in another coach. The men were given 6d. each when they promised to go to London which must have been a real adventure for them - in the company of a mad man! St. Lukes Hospital was paid £6.1s.0d. Muggleton seems to have recovered as seven months later payments to his family stopped and he and three of his sons appear in the 1841 Census return for Quy. It was an expensive illness for in two months the expenses on Muggleton's account were over £30.

CLUBS

No doubt improvements in the medical service had accounted for the improved life expectancy and the drop in infant mortality. It is clear that the overseers were helping to make these services available for those who were unable to afford them. There are two cases of money being paid to labourers so that they could keep up payments with "their club". Notices of Medical Clubs were beginning to appear in the Cambridge Chronicle by 1821. For instance, the General Benefit Insurance Company were offering from 4s. to 36s. per week during sickness with medical attendance and medicine; from £5 to £60 payable at death; and from 2s. to £2 per week in old age. Clearly the premiums for such insurance would have been well outside what a labouring man could afford but there were many locally run clubs which offered some help towards medical care and payments during illness.

Samuel Norman with the help of his family was normally self-supporting but he hit a bad patch in 1823. The overseers paid him 2s. in April and May "when his children could not stone"; he had two small payments when his wife was ill; on several occasions he was paid 1s. "to make up his allowance" which probably meant that he was getting some money for illness from his club but not enough for him to live on. As he had seven children at the time, it was probably expedient for the overseer to give him 2s.6d. in November to pay his club, as had his membership lapsed he might not have been eligible to rejoin since entry was usually restricted to the fit and healthy

12 WORK FOR THE ABLE-BODIED

Quy was essentially an agricultural village and the majority of the fit men and boys worked on the land, increasingly having their employment in the half dozen large farms. Stockmen, horsekeepers, and shepherds would have all the year round jobs. Ploughing, sowing, harrowing, with perhaps some winter hedging and ditching would have kept others employed between the busy times of harvest. Work was plentiful during haytime and harvest, but though threshing provided some casual work, there were always those who found themselves unemployed at various times in the winter months.

The 1601 Poor Law Act made it the duty of each parish not only to maintain the impotent poor but also to find work for the able-bodied. Practically the only work which they could be found was on the maintenance of roads. There are no entries relating to this in the overseers' accounts prior to 1740 when they spent 4s. when they chose the surveyors and from then on until the end of the accounts in 1744, they paid surveyors' bills and quarterage (usually about 11s.8d.). In September 1740, £1.18s. was paid for "Stone and Labror for the Iye Way"; in 1741 they entered "9 poosts for Quy Water 9s." and "15 poolls of diching at Quy Water 7s." and "for digging the rotes and spreding stones 3s.". These would perhaps be the preliminaries to opening up the Turnpike Road in 1745.

The parishioners had the right to cut turf in the Fen. It was usual for the amount cut to be regulated and all that was cut had to be carted from the fen before Christmas Day. At Swaffham Prior the practice was abused and the turf was sold out of the village (Whetham 1971). There is no mention of fen reeves being appointed in Quy to regulate the amount cut but it is possible that the unemployed made some money by selling turf within the village.

There are few instances in the 18th century accounts where it is certain that the overseers were providing work for the men, but this is mainly because most payments had no reason given. Children were taught to spin by William Mason and women were provided with wheels from time to time. The only person for whom the overseer explicitly stated that he provided work was for Ann Asplen. She turned up in the village from London in December 1734 (presumably a widow of one of the Quy Asplens) but probably preferred city life as she seems to have drifted into Cambridge on more than one occasion. In April 1737, the overseer paid "for fetchin and cartin home Asplens work 1s."; October 1737 "Providing Asplen work 1s."; 1742 "Five pounds of wooll for Ann Asplen 5s.6d." "A wheel and reale for her 4s.6d." (Watts, 1977).

A century later the amount of parish work had increased. A labourer losing a job with one farmer would have been unlikely to get one with another in the village. A man could only get any help from the Poor Law in the village in which he had a settlement, either by birth or by working for more than a year in that place. It was difficult for a man with dependants to get a settlement in another village. Four men were "diging the sides of the Road down up to the Church"; "cleaning the tunnel on Seven Acres droveway" "cleaning 60 rods of the Town river at 10d per Rod". Surveyors' accounts were always high in the winter and low in summer, so this must to some extent have helped during the slack winter months on the farm. No doubt the standard of roads had improved during the course of the past 100 years.

Often payments were made because someone was "out of work" or was "looking after work". In April 1823, for instance, Richard Medbury had 1s. "when he went after a job". For the next two months the overseer paid him 1s. a week "when working for Mr Payne to make up his allowance". This was just after Richard Ambrose had had to sell up the farm because of financial difficulties and it is likely that Medbury and four others were taken on by Mr Payne at less than the proper wage rather have them completely idle. They all had several dependent children at the time who would have to be supported from the rates if he had not found their father some employment - but probably he did not really need their labour. The number of people going to look for jobs suggests that they were having to travel out of the village, probably to Cambridge, to find work.

The allowance was not automatically paid. John Beales, for instance, had 10d "to make up his allowance by Magistrate order". In May 1823, Billy the Blacksmith had to go before the magistrates at Bottisham who ordered the overseer "to make up his allowance and if he did not work as other Men did they would send him to the House of Correction." Billy Howard had at least eleven children of whom seven died in infancy or early childhood, most births or deaths necessitating some payment from the overseers. He was often ill or out of work. In fact it was probably because of families such as this that it was "fashionably thought that allowances and wage subsidies were root causes of unwanted rural population increase as well as shiftlessness" (Marshall, 1968)

Thatched cottages which once stood near the crossroads in the centre of the village. The left one was called the Priest's Chambers. The Bishop of Ely, in exchange for the great tithes, at one time sent a priest to take an occasional service. This house was used by him then and his horse stabled there. In 1836, it was considered impossible to make it into a fit residence for an incumbent. The cottages were pulled down in 1920 when the (old) Village Hall was erected.

13 SOCIAL STRUCTURE OF QUY

There had been a change in social pattern during the 18th century. Not only had the land become more concentrated into the hands of fewer <u>owners</u> but also into the hands of fewer <u>tenants</u>. As the six farms had increased in size, the social status of the farmers had risen above that of the smallholders. The labourers became more dependent on a few large farmers for their livelihood and widows were reduced to paupers because of the lack of home industry.

Here the three groups are linked into a total village community. For brevity "ratepayers" include the farmers, smallholders and small businessmen; the "labourers" are the employed people; "paupers" are those who received regular weekly allowances from the overseers. The income from Townland, 14 acres of charity land, was distributed to what was known in those days as "the industrious poor", which consists of all those who were neither ratepayers nor paupers (see Appendix 3).

The number of ratepayers are known for the early 19th century but are less easily determined for the earlier period. However an estimate can be made from those who were nominated as overseers (plus one known shopkeeper). This could be an underestimate if, for instance, any of the ratepayers were illiterate and therefore unable to carry out the overseers' duties. A rough guide to literacy can be obtained from marriage registers after 1754. Between 1754 and 1780, half the men (46%) and half the women (52%) could at least sign their name so it is likely that most of the ratepayers were literate throughout the period we are considering. As the number of labourers grew, so did the number of illiterates. Thus for the marriages between 1801 and 1825 only about one in four (26%) of the men and one in three of the women (33%) were able to sign the register.

Of the 40 surnames in 1742, only ten appear in 1821 which suggests that there was considerable movement in and out of the village, though the high infant mortality would also cause family names to disappear. Of the 71 surnames in 1821, twenty were still in Quy 100 years later, but of these today only three remain - Flack, Wright and Chapman.

Table 5
Number of Families in the three socioeconomic groups

	Ratepayers	Labourers	Paupers	Total
1742	14 (30%)	28 (61%)	4 (9%)	46
1821	11 (11%)	70 (72%)	16 (16%)	97

Table 5 shows the number of families in the three socio-economic groups which made up the village community in 1742 and 1821. This confirms the trends already noted. Although the number of households had more than doubled the number of ratepayers had decreased from 14 to 11. The number of paupers had increased fourfold in number - or double in proportion. During 1742, eight of the labourers' families were given either money or clothes and in 1821 about the same proportion (15) labourers' families received financial help. Overall the total number of families needing help from the parish rose from 1 in 4 in 1742 to 1 in 3 in 1821.

The 1831 Census gives the number of agricultural occupiers employing labour and the number not employing labour. Again Quy shows a different pattern from Bottisham and Little Wilbraham.

Table 6
Number of agricultural occupiers in the 1831 Census

	Quy	Bottisham	L.Wilb
Occupiers employing labour	6	14	5
Occupiers not employing labour	2	42	5
Labourers	65	119	48
Average no. per farm	10.8	8.5	9.6

Quy had three times as many farmers as smallholders whereas Bottisham had three times many smallholders as farmers. Little Wilbraham had an equal number of each. Quy had the largest average labour force per farm.

Thus if there were only two smallholders and the number had dwindled considerably during the past 100 years, it could not have been the 1839 Enclosure Act which was responsible for the decline. Bottisham and Little Wilbraham had both been enclosed before 1831.

14 "PROGRESS"

In general, payments for illness were much more common in the 19th century than in the 18th century, despite the improvements in medical care. The labouring community were less able to cope with temporary setbacks than a peasant one. For instance, a cow did not stop giving milk because the owner was ill and if no other member of the family was able to milk it, a neighbour could do it - perhaps in exchange for part of the yield; a pig would provide meat for several months; women could pay a more economic part with spinning at home; more use could be made of the fen for stover or turf, particularly as the labourers' hours would have been virtually from dawn to dusk for much of the year. Larger families meant more overcrowding. The lower the standard of living the more susceptible to illness a family would be; illness led to under- or unemployment; this in turn led to reliance on the parish for relief at subsistence level; this did nothing to improve the living standards.... "Progress" had brought about a money-based economy for the lower classes; labourers had little enough money even when in good health and full employment.

Henry Burling illustrates the kind of difficulties which might be met. He seems to have been a man who was not very robust (though he lived to be 78). In August 1823, he was living in Fen Ditton when he and his family became "very dangerously ill" and a nurse had to be found by the Quy overseer to look after them. Eight payments were made to the nurse or family within three weeks. After this setback, it is perhaps not surprising that Henry could not pay his rent at Michaelmas, and he was evicted from his house. The overseer made a "Journey to Horningsey to see Burlings Landlord whose name is Cousins to redeem his bed but he refused to let me have them." The overseer gave the evicted man 1s.2½d. " when all his goods were taken away" (at the same time charging 2s.6d. for his own journey of a few miles!). Later Burling needed £2 to buy himself a bed and other necessities. A little more generosity on the part of the overseers after his serious illness might in the end have proved cheaper.

In the 18th century, the duties of overseer had been spread more widely. Though the larger farmers took their turns more frequently, others were considered eligible, and in fact did serve their community. By the 19th century, there were fewer smallholders and the level of literacy had deteriorated. Probably too, "progress" had brought about more rules and regulations for keeping the books and the amount of money involved was so much greater that only the more educated would have been able to cope. The gap between the "haves" and "have-nots" had undoubtedly widened during the century. As Bovill (1962) stated the farmers' standard of living increased but not that of the labourers. He quotes Cobbett as saying "Why do not farmers now feed and lodge their work-people as they did formerly? Because they cannot keep them on so little as they give them in wages."

Today, the standard of living is vastly improved from those of village people in the 18th century. But in this time of recession (1993), the Chancellor of the Exchequer faces the same problem that overseers up and down the country were facing then - rising prices, unemployment, welfare payments, shortage of hospital beds, road improvements, poor housing. But at least the overseers did not feel the need to concern themselves with education.

REFERENCES

Anon (1955) "The Poor of the Parish, 1760-1830 Swaffham Prior
    Cambridgeshire Local History Bulletin No.8
BOVILL,E.W. (1962) English Country Life 1780-1830 Oxford University
    Press
BURN Dr. (1814) Justices of Peace Vol. IV
Cambridge Chronicle Weekly Papers in Cambridgeshire Collection
    24.9.1886 Obituary of Rev. Ventris
CAMBRIDGESHIRE FAMILY HISTORY SOCIETY (1985) St Mary's Church, Stow
    cum Quy, Monumental Inscriptions
CHAMBERS, J.D. & MINGAY, G.E. (1966) The Agricultural Revolution 1750-
    1880 Batsford
COOPER,C.H. (1852) Annals of Cambridge Vol. 4.
County Record Office Documents
    52.6.1-14 (1726) Lease of Quy Hall Estate
    334/045 Land Tax Returns 1757-1763,1789-1837
HAMPSON,E.M. (1934) The Treatment of Poverty in Cambridgeshire
HAYWARD (1656) Original Survey of the Fens Quoted in WELLS, S. (1830)
    History of the Bedford Level
KING, Peter J. (1934) in a personal communication to Miss Francis of
    Quy Hall
Magdalen College Muniment Room Lease 22.1.1692 includes 1777 survey
    of lands in possession of John Martin, lessee
MARSHALL, J.D. (1968) The Old Poor Law 1795-1834 Studies in Economic
    History
MITCHELL, B.R. (1962) Abstract of British Historical Statistics CUP
ROYAL COMMISSION ON HISTORICAL MONUMENTS (1972) An Inventory of
    Historical Monuments in the County of Cambridge, Vol. II
    North East Cambridgeshire HMSO
SEDGWICK, Romney (1970) The History of Parliament: The House of
    Commons 1715-1754 HMSO
TAYLOR, C. C. (1973) The Cambridgeshire Landscape Houghton & Stodder
VANCOUVER, C. (1794) General View of the Agriculture in the County of
    Cambridgeshire
WATTS, Peggy (1976) Quy, 1720-1830: A Time of Change Unpublished
    (1977) "The Asplen Family of Quy" Cambridgeshire Local
    History Bulletin. No. 32
    (1993) Quy in the Mid Nineteenth Century (To be published)
WHETHAM E. (1971)" Turf Digging in Swaffham Prior in the 18th century"
    Cambridge Local History Bulletin No. 26.

APPENDIX 1

GENERAL ECONOMIC TRENDS

In the early 18th century accounts of the Quy overseers, total yearly payments rose from around £20 to a peak of £60 in 1729, fell back to around £30 and then peaked again in 1741 before once more falling (see Fig. 2).

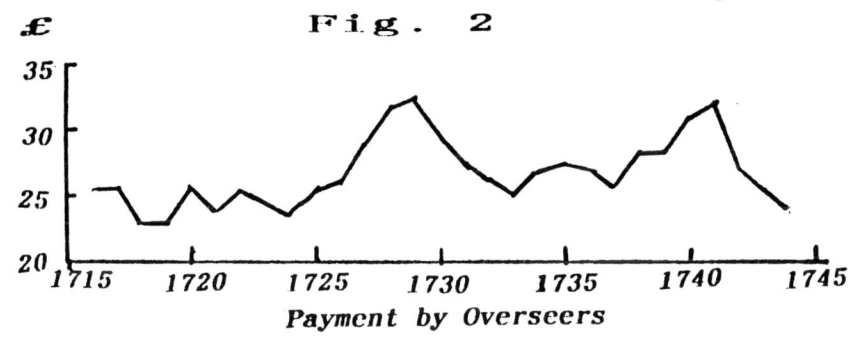

Fig. 2

Payment by Overseers

It must be significant that the only two years in which wheat was imported into Britain during the first half of the 18th century were 1728-9 and 1740-1 (Mitchell, 1962) After only a few years of poor harvests, wheat would become scarce and very dear, affecting not only the farmers but also the lower classes who would pay dearly for their staple diet of bread and would be short of work in the winter if there were less threshing.

The 19th century overseers' book runs from 1817 to 1830 but the last year's accounts may be incomplete. It can be seen on Fig. 3 that the amount per year distributed was around £300, being particularly high during 1817.

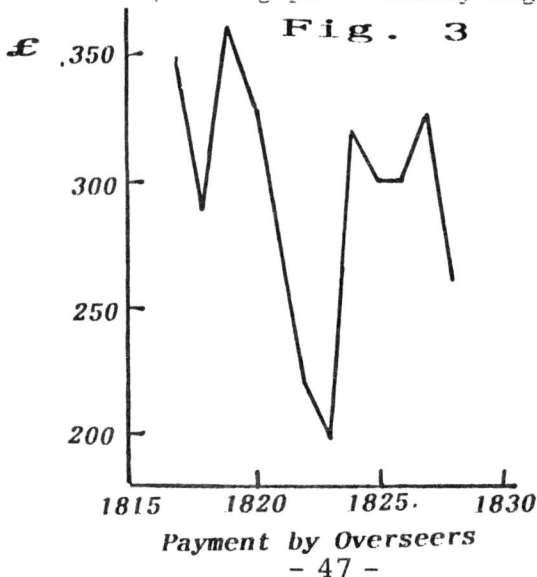

Fig. 3

Payment by Overseers

1819,1820 (over £330) and low in 1822 and 1823 (£223 and £198 respectively). By this time a considerable amount of wheat was being imported every year but it is interesting that when the imports of wheat into Great Britain rose above 1m. qrs of wheat, (Mitchell, 1962) the Quy overseers expenditure was above £300.

The 19th century accounts do include the totals (but no details) of the constables' and surveyors' bills but these represent only about 25% of the total amount paid out. In any case, the surveyors provided income for those who were able to work but who were without employment (Whetham, 1955) so if the men had not been paid for work on the roads, the overseers would have had to support their families.

Public spending nationally between 1714 and 1740 ranged from £4.6m and £7.1m, being £6.2m in both 1714 and 1740, but increasing by 50% between 1741-1744. By 1816 national public spending was £79.1m, dropping the following two years as Britain recovered from the Napoleonic Wars. For the next 12 years it fluctuated between £54.7m and £61.6m. Thus it can be seen that the parish figures of a tenfold increase over the 100 years or so are mirrored in the national figures.

Consumer goods however had risen much less. The high prices of the Napoleonic Wars were over by 1818. Meat was roughly three times as dear in the 1820s as in 1750 (rising from approx. 1s. to 3s per stone). Wheat prices fluctuated greatly according to the harvest but were normally around 30s. per quarter in the first half of the 18th century and about twice as high in the 1820s. The price of bread in London had varied from 4d. to 6½d. throughout the earlier period and had risen to 9½d-10½d per 4 lb. in the 1820s (Chambers & Mingay, 1966). The Schumpter-Gilbey price indices for consumer goods (embracing food stuffs, drinks, candles and clothing) based on 1701 = 100, shows the index rising above 100 only six times in the 1714-1744 period (the two highest being 104 in 1729 and 108 in 1741, which were the peak years in the overseers' accounts) whereas the index was below 90 for ten of these years (lowest 84 in 1714). The equivalent figures are only given to the year 1823 and show a steady fall from 194 in 1818 to 125 in 1822 (128 in 1823). Thus increase in price of commodities was a comparatively minor matter.

Marshall (1968) gives the average <u>per capita</u> relief expenditure on the poor in 1821 as 10s.6d nationally and 14s.9d. in Cambridgeshire, one of the counties most affected by the agricultural depression. Quy overseers paid out 14s.9d. <u>per capita</u> (12s.1d. when the surveyors' accounts etc. are deducted). Thus the depression was no worse here than in the rest of the county and may have been offset to some extent by the nearness of Cambridge where some of the industrious able-bodied may have found work. The social structure had changed and this had added to the strains on the Parish rates.

APPENDIX 2

John Arbrow

John Arbrow (variously spelt Arbor, Arborough, Arborow, Arborows) first appeared in Quy Parish Registers as the father of Mary, baptised 26th March 1721. A son, John, born in 1723 died 3 months after being baptised, and a second John born the following year died in March 1726. The mother of the children, Sarah, had died in December 1725. It is not recorded in the Quy Registers when John married Ann, but he himself died in June 1734 - a month before Ann's daughter Ann was baptised.

Perhaps because he died about the time Ann was giving birth to her daughter, who was buried on 26th August, the inventory of his goods was not made immediately and is dated 6th November 1734, by which time the harvest had been gathered in. The inventory was signed on 23rd November 1734 by Richard Brand and by the mark of Thomas Challis. His widow was sworn to the truth of the inventory. The value of "his wearing apparel and money in his purse £1.1s." is somewhat lower than one might expect - perhaps due to the passage of time?

The inventory shows that the Arbrows lived in a 8-roomed house with a separate dairy, furnished as follows:

In the Lower Chamber a Hutch a Chest fire shovels & tongs &
 brass bellows and Linning in the Chest 9 Sheets 2 tablecloths
 23 Knapkins and fouer pillowbeers   £3. 0s. 0d
In the Little Room 6 Chayers & one table   7s. 0d
In the Parlour one featherbed & bedstead a pair of sheets
 one blanket one quilt one piller one bolster   £1. 10s. 0d
 A chest of drawers 5 Chayers one looking glass
 one little table   £1. 10s. 0d
In another Chamber one bed one blanket & a bedstead   2s. 6d
In another Chamber One feather bed & bedstead a Coverhead   10s. 6d
In the Cellar 4 small Vessels 2 tubbs a kneeding trough
 & one sieve   8s. 0d
In the Hall House 3 large pouter Dishes 8 small ones 14 plates
 a Dresser & Pewter Case 2 Kettells a Chafin dish 2 tables
 8 Chayres fire shovel & tongs bellows & Gridiron a jack &
 Lock Iron 3 Candel sticks a Warming pan one Spyt Stilyards
 & peet   £2. 1s. 0d
In another Room a porridge pott & frying pan   12s. 6d
In the Dayrey one cheese press 4 Shelves a Stand keeler
 & other things   12s. 6d

The value of the farming goods place him into the top 40% of the existing Quy inventories so he probably had a medium sized farm. He had 3 mares and one foal, 4 cows and 2 calves and 2 hogs. By November the corn had already been thrashed and in the barn were barley £20; wheat and rye £15.2s.; a deal of flour £1.10s. and lentils £2. The tilling of the land was appraised at £7, dung £2 and "hay abroad" £3. There were also the usual farm implements

By December 1735, John's widow Ann had married Roger Smith and she then swore to the truth of an account of the money she had spent paying any outstanding debts and "Inning the Crops growing" which had been valued after they were in the barns in November 1734, and not as they were at the time of John's death. This gives valuable information about the pay for harvest work in 1734.

29 Aug	Francis Taborham for reaping of two acres of wheat	8s. 0d
10 Sep	George Morgan for two Days in Harvest	2s. 0d
	Wm Johnson for his Harvest wages	£1. 10s. 6d
30 Sep	John Rayment & his Earnest	£2. 1s. 0d
	Wm Johnson for 6 Days threshing by the day	6s. 0d
	Shop goods that was used in Harvest	10s. 6d
	Sack carrying & Toll & other expenses of 3 loads of wheat	3s. 6d
1 Oct	Wm Johnson for Threshing & Dressing of 10 qrs Wheat	15s. 0d
	Brooms & Wings	1s. 0d
	Wm Johnson for a days work when the wheat was carried out	10d

On 18 February 1735, Francis Whybrow was paid 19s.2d for "dung and ditching" and William Whybrow 2s.4d for ditching. In September 1734, Wm Ames was paid £3.2s.0d "on the Horse Fair Day" but whether this was in payment of a debt or his wages as a horsekeeper can only be guessed. 1s. was paid for a halter and expenses when the colt was sold, and 6d expenses when the cow was sold. Other expenses are likely to be rent: Johns College £10 in October and £5 the following April; Bennet College £1.18s.10d; Thomas Halfhyde £11. Richard Brand, who signed the inventory was paid 3s.7d "for writing and stamp paper" on 1st October 1734 - more than a month before the inventory was drawn up. On the same day 3d was paid for a letter from Mr Robinson, London, and Oliver Robinson was paid £2 on 18th February 1835. Thomas Challis, who signed with his mark, was paid £8. 19s.0d in February 1735 which could perhaps have been his wages. Thomas Leech received 2s.8d for 14 lb. beef but the "Diet for the servants" was only £2 (could this be for a year?). A number of other amounts remain unexplained, e.g. "Matthew Muncey £5,5s."

John Arbrow's funeral expenses and those of his baby daughter (dated 17 May 1735) were:

Robert Mansfield for a Coffin	16s. 0d
For burying suit & gloves	£1. 1s. 0d
For Cakes	4s. 0d
For Two Nurses that laid him out	4s. 0d
Pd the clerk	11s. 6d
Pd for 2 Affidavits	1s. 0d
Funeral expenses for the child	
for a coffin	16s. 0d
for burying suit and gloves	3s. 7d
to Stephen Chevers	1s. 6d
Pd for laying out the child	1s. 0d
for a burying cloth	2s. 0d

The expenses charged by the widow amounted to £79.15s.2d. The total value of the inventory was £89.4s. of which £10.13s.6d was for the household goods.

APPENDIX 3

Townland or Childe's Charity

In 1675, John Childe conveyed 10 acres of arable land to the Churchwardens and Overseers of Quy in fulfilment of the wishes of his grandfather Robert Lawrence of Quy Hall who had died before the bequest had been settled. The profits of the land were originally paid quarterly to ten of the poor.

According to the 1837 Charity Commissioners report, the 1786 returns mention "that there was then some land, the donor of which was unknown, the rent thereof, amounting to £2 per annum, was appropriated for the use of the poor not in receipt of relief". Between 1733 and 1744 a (damaged) book shows £2 being paid every other year, though it is not clear what the relation was between Mr Martin and the Rent. For instance, one page is headed

> "Jan. 26 1736 then paid to the poor....
> which was due from William Hovill for four A...
> One Rood of some land at St Michal(ma)s La..."

This is followed by a list of 20 names receiving amounts between 1s. and 3s.6d, totalling £2. At the bottom of the same page there is an entry:

> "Apl the 11 1737 received two years Intrust money
> of Esq. Martin £2 Due Lady Day last per Thos. Muggleton"

Thus these two lots of land together made up 14a. 1r. and this was let to Richard Webb in 1731 when the Overseer drew up the following Memorandum

> "Richard Weebb of Stow Cum Qui doth enter upon fourteen acres and a rood of town land belonging to the poor of the parish att the yearly rent of Six pounds ten Shilings And the S(ai)d Rich(ar)d Weeb do agree to lay Thirty good loads of muck every year upon some part of the s(ai)d lande. And for the term of six years"

The land was scattered among the open strips in the three open fields. The rent was then 9s an acre in 1731 but William Hovill paid 10s. some ten years later.

A later Townland book exists which shows rents were considerably higher at the end of the Napoleonic Wars. From 1819-1821 the rent was £2.9s. an acre; in 1822 £2.1s.6d. in 1823-24 £1.18s.; and from 1825-1833 had dropped to £1.1s. According to Chambers & Mingay (1966) rents generally doubled between 1793 and 1815 and then fell until 1835 when they again rose. In a parish near Ely, the rent trebled between 1791 and 1820 from 10s. to 30s; Rates from 2s. in £ to 12s.; and agricultural taxes from £91 to £343. Labour costs had risen from 1s.-1s.3d. per to 1s.6d. to 2s. (Cambridge Chronicle 23.1.1821)

The Townland rent in 1826 was double that quoted by Vancouver in 1794 but in the early 1820s they had reached five times the 1794 rate. It is interesting that in 1821-2 the land was rented by Ambrose, the second largest landowner in the village; in 1822 the land was rented by one of the smallholders; and in 1823 by another. From 1826, the Townland was shared by eight different smallholders. Thus as the rent went down the land passed from the hands of one large farmer to an number of small, part-time ones.

From the income of Townland, Poor Rate tax had to be paid, and the Eau Brink Drainage on the Common Fen was deducted. The remainder of the income was distributed to those families who were neither ratepayers nor in receipt of parish relief. The amount each family received depended on the number of people in the household. Lists remain for the years 1819-1823 when approx. 270 people received money each year.

Page from the 1821 Townland Account Book

No	Names	£ . s . d
6 at 3/6	John Flack	1 . 1 . 0
2	W Daisley	0 . 7 . 0
6	Parker	1 . 1 . 0
2, 1	D Iron	0 . 7 . 0
7	J Iron	1 . 4 . 6
6	T House	1 . 1 . 0
8	T Reeve	
2	H Carter	0 . 7 . 0
2	J Dean	0 . 7 . 0
2	H Smgglton	0 . 7 . 0
2	J Flower	0 . 7 . 0
3	H Iron	0 . 10 . 6
2	W Wolf	0 . 7 . 0
5	W Littlechild	0 . 17 . 6
3	J Langham	0 . 10 . 6

- 52 -

Year requesth the accounts of Richard
Well overseers for the poor of Quy

Com Quy April 5 Day 1724		
Paid for the ditcations ———	0 2	6
Quy giving to Bottisham townsend	0 1	0
Paid 3 Widow Tompson ———	0 0	11
Paid Widow Tompson ———	1	8
Paid Widow Newman 4 weeks Colection	4	0
Paid Widow Clark 4 weeks Colection	2	-5
Paid a Widow Tompson ———	0	5
for a new Smock for the Widow Tompson	2	6
Paid Widow Clark in sickens	1	0
Paid Widow Clark in sickens	0	6
Paid Widow Clark in sickens	0	11

Extract from the Quy Overseers' Accounts for 1724

INDEX OF SURNAMES

Adams/Adames 20 24
Alling 12
Ambrose 12 13 17 18
    40 41 51
Ames 50
Arber 27
Arbor/Arborough/
    Arborow/Arbrow 35
    49 50
Asplen/Asplin 20 23
    25 35 36 40
Aylesford Lord 13

Banks 12
Beales 41
Benson 29
Bett 16
Bowtell 36
Brand 49 50
Bridgman 21
Briggs 24
Brooks 30
Burling 26 44
Butler 26 27 28
Byford 29

Carter 32 52
Challis 28
Chapman 22 36 43
Childe 51
Chivers/Chevers 28
Claksen 23
Clark/Clarke 21 37
Cocks 35 36
Cole 12 18
Collett 17 19
Collier 13
Cook 28 29
Cotton 13
Course 52
Cousins 44
Culledge 12
Cullifer/Culliver 25
Curtis 14 16 23

Daisley 52
Davis 34
Dean 52
Dobson 17 18 30
Dossiter 21

Edwards 20 21
Ellis 17 19
Ester 25

Farrow 12 14 15 24 25
Flack 13 19 43 52
Flower 52
Foote 14 16 35
Fordham 26

Gillam 33

Halfehide/Halfhyde 12
    50
Harrison 11
Hattley/Hattly 25
Herring 11
Hicks 11 18 31
Hovill 14 15 16 23
    35 51
Howard 29 41
Howlett 16 20

Ison 8 16 30 52

Jenyns/Jennings 8 13
    15 18 24
Johnson 35 36 50

Kerridge 22

Langham 52
Lawrence 37 55
Leech 50
Littlechild 52

Mallion 29
Manning 27
Mansfield 50
Marsh 38
Martin 2 4 10 12 13
    14 15 16 19 51
Mason 24 39
Medbury 40
Moore 16
Morgan 35 50
Muggleton 8 12 14 23
    25 31 32 35 37 38
    51 52
Mumford 37
Muncey 50
Munns 26

Newman/Numan 4 21 23
    28 31 36 37 53
Noble 21
Norman 38

Okes 37
Osborn 33
Oslar/Ostler 16 21

Parr/Pur 16
Parker 52
Paul 17
Payne 17 19 40
Pemberton 18
Piper 16 21
Pratt 36
Preston 26
Prince 17 19 22 27 36

Raby 16
Randall/Randle 13 29
Rant 11 33 34
Rayment 50
Reed/Reeve 21 25 52
Robinson 50
Russell 23
Rycroft 12

Sericold 12
Sewell 16
Shipp 37
Smith 22 23 24

Taborham 50
Tag 28
Taylor 16
Thomson/Tompson/
    Tomson 20 21 25 32
    53

Unwin 30

Ventris 11

Webb/Weeb 14 15 28 51
    53
Wells 36
Wheeler 32
Whichcote 10
White 27
Whybrow/Wibrow/Wybrow
    24 25 50
Wolf 52
Wright 43

Yorke 24 25